THE TEEN SURVIVAL GUIDE

Copyright©2015.The Teen Survival Guide. Jonathan Mashack All Rights Reserved. No part of this book may be reproduced or transmitted in any form or by any means without the permission in writing from the publisher. Published by Holy Cow Book Publishers

CONTENTS

Introduction	5
How to Use	7
Life	11
Mindsets	19
Self-Esteem	27
Staying Out of Trouble	33
Making Good Decisions	37
Staying Focused	43
Relationships	47
Parents	55
Anger	59
Bullying	69
Sex	77
Conclusion	89

INTRODUCTION

This book is designed for all young adults who want to grow mentally, emotionally, and even spiritually. I am more than confident that if you apply the principles from this book to your life, you will grow better every day. You can do more than survive your teenage years, you can also thrive!

So, if you are looking to improve your life, then you've come to the right place. Apply the principles in this book, and you will see a positive change.

Why I HAD to Write This Book

During my first year of teaching high school, three students tragically lost their lives (two of the three were suicides). I didn't know the students, but their deaths had deeply impacted me. So, I prayed about what I could do to prevent my students from making the same or similar decisions. I was led to share the life skills that I've acquired over the years with my students. I did it at the start of every class. After doing this for several weeks, one of my students began to call them, "Serious Tips."

After giving daily tips consistently, not only did I see a difference in classroom behavior but also in the student's personal lives. I even found out that several of my students ended up changing their minds about committing suicide because of these tips. After seeing how the serious tips impacted my students, I contemplated compiling the tips into a book.

Not long after, several students requested that I compile the tips into a book. The fact that they requested it confirmed things for me and ultimately helped me decide to move forward with publishing this very book, *The Teen Survival Guide*.

I'd like to give a very special thanks to those students who encouraged me to follow through with this publication.

__HOW TO USE__

The Guide to Navigating the Teen Survival Guide.

YOUNG ADULTS

Pre-teens and young adults, I've created this book with you in mind. The Teen Survival Guide can be utilized in multiple ways:

A Daily Devotional

You can use this book like a devotional, reading only one tip daily, and apply what you've read when the opportunity presents itself. The idea is to have solutions to your problems before the problems ever arrive. Once you've read all of the tips, start over again, especially if you failed to apply some of them to your life before. Also, participate in the challenges throughout the book.

A Guide for Specific Issues

This book is full of answers to many questions about how you should approach various situations. Let's say that you have a problem, you don't know how to handle it. All you have to do is pick a topic from the contents

8 | TEEN SURVIVAL GUIDE

and read within that section until you find the answer. If you don't find the answer that you need, just search for it on a different topic.

TEACHERS

Teachers, you can use this book the same way that I did when I was a teacher. The idea was to begin each of my classes on a positive note by telling my students one serious tip that could benefit them in their everyday lives. **NOTE:** *These tips would also help students to refocus their minds by leaving behind their previous troubles from before they've entered my classroom.*

Not only will the students appreciate the consistency of daily positivity, but they'll also appreciate the love that they feel when they realize that you're doing this specifically for their well-being. The only thing that you should be mindful of is that: ***some of the tips are NOT appropriate for the classroom.*** So use them at your own discretion.

MENTORS

As a mentor, you can use this book as a segway to begin a dialogue between yourself and your mentee. Allow them to share their opinions about the contents of the book and discuss it further in a meaningful conversation. Even see if they've had to deal with any of the problems mentioned in the book. This book can help tear down the walls blocking communication between you and your mentee.

Another option is to simply share daily tips with them as a way to show that you are concerned about their well-being.

PARENTS/GUARDIANS

Parents and Guardians may also use this book in the same way as the Mentor but with fewer boundaries. Using it as a way to start a conversation. When doing this you must be consistent. You can even schedule a special time for you and your teen to discuss the contents of the book. **NOTE:** *In this process try to be a listener with an open heart, try to be slow to anger, and try to be slow to judge. This process takes vulnerability. I encourage you to talk about your life when you* *were a teen and how you can relate to the things that they are going through. Allow them to see that you've made mistakes while also showing that those mistakes had consequences.*

Another way to use this book is to read it as if you are an adolescent and apply the principles to your life. Doing this will allow you to lead by example. Sometimes the best motivation for a young adult is to see a positive change made in their parents.

LIFE

Life is unpredictable. The sun shines on everyone, but, at the same time, the rain pours on everyone, too. In other words, we all have good and bad times. With that being said, why have more bad times than you have to?

When you make poor choices based on negativity, you get negative results. So, why not make positive choices?

Applying the tips from this section will help you be better prepared for a variety of trials that may occur in your everyday life.

12 | TEEN SURVIVAL GUIDE

1. KEEP RUNNING
In the story "The Tortoise and the Hare," the tortoise refused to stop running even though it looked as if he could not win the race. Nonetheless, he continued running and ended up winning the race. If he had given up, he would not have had the opportunity to win.

So, I encourage you to keep running. Even if it doesn't look like you have a chance to win in life. If you endure, you may be pleasantly surprised when you make it to your finish line.

2. BEING NEW
When you are in an unfamiliar situation or new environment (which can be a little scary), pay close attention to your surroundings. Look for the following:
- Things you are expected to do and know;
- Things you should not do or say;
- People you should stay away from;
- People that you can relate to (or potential friends)

3. LIFE
Life is what you make it, so choose your ingredients wisely: Anger, Fear, Hate, Love, Joy, Bitterness, and Peace, which

ingredients will you choose?

REMEMBER: Life can give you a lot of bad circumstances, but those circumstances don't determine what ingredients you choose to have in your life. You can choose to be a loving person in a hateful environment.

4. LISTEN TO WISE COUNSEL
It is better to be corrected by one wise person than to be praised by many fools. Justification is the only reason a fool will praise another, but the wise is concerned for your life.

5. POWERFUL OR PITIFUL
I once heard Joyce Meyer say, "You can be Powerful or Pitiful, but you can't be both." In other words, you have to make a decision to let things go. Otherwise, you could allow one thing to hold you back for the rest of your life.

6. PATIENCE
When you have patience, you find that you are less aggravated with people. With patience comes better health and peace of mind. To be patient just means that you can tolerate delay (or waiting) without getting upset.

7. DOING YOUR BEST

No matter what you are doing, always put your best foot forward, even if you don't like doing it. If someone sees that you'll do a good job on something that you don't like doing, they'll be quicker to hire you to do something that you love.

CONSIDER THIS: I once worked for a company that paid me less than enough to get by. Instead of being bitter and not doing my job to the best of my ability, I did my job as if I was getting paid three times more than I was. A seemingly random customer came in, I helped her, and she immediately recognized my work ethic. She offered me a job on the spot paying four times the amount that I was being paid.

8. KNOWLEDGE

Knowledge is like money: the more you obtain, the more options you have. Think about it like this: if you only have $10 and you want to go out to eat, you'll have a very limited amount of restaurants to choose from, probably places with a dollar menu. On the other hand, if you have $1,000 you could pretty much eat out wherever you want. It's the same with knowledge. When you have more knowledge, you can choose several paths instead of being limited.

CONSIDER THIS: If your job gave you a company car, they could take it back at any moment, but if your job taught you something valuable, they can never take that back.

9. YOUR TIME

Use your time wisely. People often say that you have 24 hours a day to complete your tasks, but that's not true if you have a healthy sleep schedule. You actually have about 16 hours a day to do whatever it is that needs to be done, assuming you don't have a job or go to school. Use your time wisely. Ask yourself, "What is taking up most of my time, and is it beneficial to my long-term or short-term goals?" If it's not, replace that thing (or activity) with something productive that will help you reach your goals."

10. STORM WARNING

Just like the clouds darken before rain, you will receive a warning before pain.

The pain I am speaking of is caused by your own actions (or poor choices). I've found that sometimes in life you'll get several warnings before your actions cause you to get into major trouble. Trouble could range from suspension to expulsion, or a bad break up, or it could even be life-threatening. So, be careful because this message may be your final warning before the storm.

11. TEMPTATION
Whenever you are tempted to do wrong, there is ALWAYS an escape (or a way out). NEVER forget that! Always take the first way out as soon as the opportunity presents itself.

12. TEMPTATION II
To avoid falling into temptation, don't put yourself in a compromising situation.

If going to a particular location will be tempting for you, just don't go. Make good choices, and you'll get good results.

KEEP IN MIND: Sometimes when you decide not to put yourself in a compromising or tempting situation, people will accuse you of not having enough willpower, but you are actually practicing your willpower and intelligence by not putting yourself in that situation. So, don't believe the accusers, and don't allow them to tempt you even further.

13. WHAT HAPPENS WHEN YOU DECIDE TO DO WHAT'S RIGHT

Sometimes when you make a conscious decision to live right (or make good choices), you are tempted to do wrong more than ever. I tell you this so that you'll be prepared and not submit to temptation.

REMEMBER: You are not tempted because you're a bad person, but you do become a better person after resisting temptation.

14. COMMITMENT

When you commit yourself to something, don't take it lightly. Don't go back on your word, and never agree to something that you are not sure that you can handle. Why? Because this is a reflection of your character. If people can't trust your word (what you say), then they probably won't trust you. It's likely that they'll tell others not to trust you as well, ruining your reputation.

15. THE TESTS

I've found that in life, you will be tested, and if you do not pass the test, you'll eventually have to take the same test over again. That's why you sometimes find yourself in the same bad situation over and over again or getting in trouble about the same thing over and over again. You haven't passed the test.

REMEMBER: If it didn't work the first time, it probably won't work the second time. Just learn from your mistakes. If you don't know how to handle a recurring problem or situation, just ask someone like a parent, pastor, teacher, or mentor for help.

16. JUST LIVE

If things are going badly and you can't see how life could get better for you, just live. Live to see how things get better. Nowadays, it seems common for someone to think about suicide at some point in his or her life. I implore you, don't even consider it! You matter; your presence makes a difference even if you can't see it right now. Even when you don't open your mouth, your presence is impacting the people around you. So, live until you see things get better. Just live.

MINDSETS

The way you think will reveal itself in the things you do and in the things you say. In fact, your actions and your lifestyle are a direct reflection of your mindset (or your thoughts). If you have a positive mindset, you'll make positive decisions, but if you have a negative mindset you will make negative decisions. Knowing this, you now have the ability to reprogram your mind to think more positively than negatively.

You might think that you don't know how to reprogram your mind, but you already do it on a regular basis. Think about it like this; have you ever had a class with someone who was annoying? If so, before going to that class you may have thought things like, 'If they say anything to me today, I'm going to give them a piece of my mind.' Then, when you get to the class, you give that person a piece of your mind because they said the wrong thing.

When you thought about giving that person a piece of your mind, you were programming your mind to tell them off. In the same way, we can reprogram our mind to think thoughts like: 'No matter how annoying that person is, I will not be bothered by them.' Reprogramming your mind doesn't usually happen overnight; it takes consistent effort. I implore you to keep trying until you see the change that you're striving for. The following tips will help to develop a more positive mindset.

1. ARE YOU WILLING TO LET GO?
It is healthy to have goals, but in order for you to reach or accomplish those goals, you must be willing to let go of something. For instance, if you want to be healthier or lose weight, you must be willing to let go of unhealthy foods or relaxing when you could be exercising.

CHALLENGE:
Ask yourself the following questions and determine what you are willing to let go of:
(1) What are your goals?
(2) What would you have to let go of in order to reach your goal?

2. MINDSETS

Your mindset is the foundation of your life. It determines if you will stand or fall during a storm. Evaluate yourself. Have you been able to remain peaceful in tough situations? If not, it is a mindset issue. Think about what you spend most of your time thinking about. If your thoughts are negative, then change them to something positive. Just in case you didn't know, you can control your own thoughts. You don't have to think about whatever pops into your mind.

3. THANKFULNESS

There is a great saying that I heard: "Your attitude is a direct reflection of your gratitude." So, be grateful for where you are in life and what you have. If you can appreciate where you are, then you will really appreciate where you are going.

CHALLENGE: The next time you catch yourself having a bad attitude, begin thinking about everything that you are grateful for and write them all down (list at least 25 things).

4. THANKFULNESS II

Be grateful even in your uncomfortable circumstances. CONSIDER THIS: Even if you don't have everything you want, you more than likely have everything that you need.

5. INTEGRITY

It is great if you behave for your parents, teachers, etc. but what do you do when they are not around? Being good in public and bad in private usually ends with everything that was in the darkness coming to light.

6. CRITICISM

When someone criticizes us, it's our decision to make it constructive or destructive. No one likes to be criticized, but we must look past our pain (or our pride) and hear how we can improve.

KEEP IN MIND: Sometimes people criticize you just to make themselves feel better. Your job is to recognize when the criticism is valuable (this takes humility and maturity).

7. BEING A LIAR

Constantly lying can ruin your reputation and may cause you to develop a lying mentality. A lying mentality is when you not only lie to others but also lie to yourself which leads to even more problems.

Most of the time, when you are honest, you'll usually be respected even if you did something that you are ashamed of. Everyone makes mistakes and people often forgive mistakes but it's very hard to believe someone who is known as a liar.

8. CHECK YOUR MOTIVES
You could be doing a good deed but for the wrong reasons. The reasons are more important than the deed. Check your motives.

9. WHAT ARE WE LISTENING TO?
Our mind believes what we say more than we believe anyone else. When we listen to music, we chant the lyrics, which subconsciously convinces us that the words in the song are the truth.

So, the question is this: "What are we listening to?" Is it helping us to develop a positive mindset or a negative mindset? If what you are listening to encourages you to speak negatively about yourself, others, or at all, then it's time for you to change what you are listening to. Especially if you want a mindset that will help you in reaching your goals.

10. FIRST REACTIONS
What is your first reaction to an unexpected situation? When someone falls, is your first reaction to laugh, or is it to help them up? Try to make your first reaction one that is

beneficial to the situation not just to yourself.

11. LETTING GO
Some people will use their past as motivation for their future while others allow their past to hold them back and keep them in bondage.

Don't let your past indicate (or determine) your future. If it is not relevant to your movement forward, leave it behind. This may seem insensitive, but it doesn't benefit you to live in the past.

12. PATIENCE WITH PEOPLE
Just because someone's not good at the same thing that you are good at doesn't mean that they're not good at something else. So, don't ever think less of anyone because they can't do something that you can do.

CONSIDER THIS: That same person who can't do what you can do probably knows how to do something that you would struggle with.

13. LOVE VS. MONEY
A lot of people die chasing money and miss out on love.

CONSIDER THIS: Imagine how you'd feel if you lost all of the money you have and compare that feeling to losing everyone that you love (i.e. friends and family). Which is the greater loss? Now, which is more important to you, love or money?

14. EVERYONE IS NOT AGAINST YOU

It's quite arrogant to think that everyone is out to get you. Do you really think that you are so special that everyone in your life is thinking of new ways to bring you down? Even though your emotions may tell you that everyone is against you or even out to get you, don't believe that lie. Sometimes when people treat you wrong, they do it unintentionally, without even knowing that their actions had any effect on you.

15. YOU ARE NOT HOW THEY TREAT YOU

At 19 years old, when I was first getting started, I tried to get an opinion about my very first children's book from a childcare director. I knocked on the door, and she looked at me through the glass window and shouted, "NO SOLICITING!" Even when she cracked the door open, and I told her that I just wanted her opinion of my very first book, she threatened to call the police on me. My motives were right, and I did not do anything illegal or wrong. Yet she treated me like a criminal.

My point is this: when she saw me, she did not see my personality or my motives. Her perception of me was no more than a stereotype due to a poor mindset. Although people may treat you like something that you are not, remember who you are.

16. REJECT BAD THOUGHTS
Everyone has bad thoughts that pop into their minds at least occasionally. So, when those bad thoughts come, don't ponder or dwell on them, but instead reject them immediately! Whenever something lustful, perverted, hateful, arrogant, devious, or just something flat-out bad, pops into your mind, tell yourself: "This is not who I am; these are not my thoughts. This is just temptation trying to poison my mind, and I refuse to be a victim!" Then, purposely start thinking good thoughts. Remember: Thoughts are the foundation of your actions, so be mindful of what you are thinking about.

SELF-ESTEEM

If you don't love yourself, how could you properly love anyone else? Chances are, if you are critical of yourself, then you are also critical of others. You may not be as critical to them as you are to yourself but it's still unhealthy.

All I'm saying is that not loving yourself develops problems in other aspects of your life. Because "you" are always everywhere you go. You can't run from yourself! Loving the skin you are in for some people requires developing a healthier way of thinking about your true identity. So, this section is designed to help you love and appreciate who you are.

28 | TEEN SURVIVAL GUIDE

1. WHO ARE YOU?
Don't let a peer's existence or status define your own.

CHALLENGE:
In order to understand yourself better answer the following questions:
      (1) What kind of person do I want to become?
      (2) What are my core beliefs?
      (3) What are you willing to fight for?

2. PUTTING YOURSELF ON DISPLAY
Present yourself in the same manner that you want to be treated. If you dress like a bum, people will treat you like one. If you speak like a dummy, people will treat you like one. Be yourself, and present yourself respectfully as you are on the inside.

3. SAYING "I CAN'T"
Sometimes saying, "I can't" is another way of saying, "I don't want to try and fail." Don't allow fear to hold you back from your full potential. Who you were yesterday is not who you are today. You get better and better as time goes by. So, exercise the full extent of your capabilities and say, "I CAN!"

At least try.

4. IT'S ALREADY IN YOU
Remind yourself that you already have everything you need to reach your goals and be successful. It's already inside you, all you have to do is use it.

5. WHAT ARE YOU SAYING?
You can convince yourself that you are not smart if you say it enough. Make sure that the words that you speak are positive, especially when you are talking about yourself.

REMEMBER: You are constantly programming your mind with your words and thoughts so make them positive, even when regarding yourself.

6. COMPLIMENTS
Anytime that you have the opportunity to sincerely compliment someone, do it! Blessing others with your words is a blessing to you.

REMEMBER: Don't give compliments just so that others can compliment you. Make sure that you keep your compliments sincere. Otherwise, you will feel bad when others don't return the compliment.

7. DON'T BEAT YOURSELF UP

We all make mistakes. So, instead of dwelling on your past mistakes, move on and do better next time. Mistakes are meant to make us better, not keep us in bondage.

8. YOU ARE VALUABLE

Just like we have cases to protect our mobile devices, we need to take care of ourselves in the same way. Don't do anything that could potentially harm you physically, mentally, or emotionally.

9. HAPPINESS II

Things cannot give us true happiness, joy, or peace. So, try making someone else happy, and see if that brings you a sense of happiness.

CHALLENGE:
The next time that you are in a bad mood, go out of your way to make someone else feel good and see how it affects you.

10. YOU ARE LOVED

Even when you've done nothing to deserve it, even if you don't know who they are, someone, somewhere, cares about you.

REMEMBER: Just because you don't feel loved does not mean that you aren't loved.

11. LIKE A CAT STUCK IN A TREE

I've never seen any cat fall that did not land safely on its feet. So, when I see a cat stuck in a tree I wonder, "Why don't they just jump?" I realize that they don't jump because of fear. They fear that they'll fall even though one of the things that makes them powerful is that they always land on their feet.

I believe that we as humans sometimes act like a cat stuck in a tree. We have everything we need to be successful or to get out of a bad situation, but sometimes we are so fearful and don't even recognize our own power and we end up remaining stuck like a cat in a tree.

I personally believe that God has already given everyone who reads this everything that they need and that they are designed for greatness.

STAYING OUT OF TROUBLE

Sometimes staying out of trouble can be hard, especially if you're used to being in trouble. This section gives you practical tips on how to keep your nose clean and out of trouble.

1. THE POWER OF SILENCE
When a person of authority asks you to do something, don't try to explain why you weren't already doing it or try to defend yourself. Just do what they asked, and it'll make your time with them a lot easier.

2. IN THE GRAY
Be black or be white (be good or be bad). When you step in and out of black and white you are in the gray. Being in the gray leads you to the bad side. Stay out of the gray.

3. REDIRECTING YOUR ENERGY

If you have a bad habit, redirect that energy to something positive. For instance, if you used to gossip, redirect those same qualities to something positive/productive like researching, studying, or becoming a salesperson. Turn your flaw into an asset.

CHALLENGE:
Think about the thing (or flaw) that usually gets you into trouble. Then brainstorm and research some positive things that you can do with that so-called flaw.

4. DON'T LET PRIDE GET IN THE WAY

There have been times when I have been given an opportunity to be relieved from the discipline that I deserved. But instead of taking the opportunity, I allowed my pride to get in the way, and I rejected the offers given to me, all because I wanted control.

Don't allow your pride to get in the way of a good opportunity. Your pride will make what was meant for a moment last a lifetime. EXAMPLE: If a teacher asks you to apologize instead of getting detention, and you refuse, then you are letting pride get in the way.

5. PICK YOUR BATTLES

Everything that offends you is not worth fighting about. With some things, it is necessary to stand your ground, but sometimes you need to just let it go. Especially if you prefer peace over strife.

6. LIKE A SPONGE

We as humans adapt to our surroundings. That's why we have to be careful about the people we hang with or associate with because we'll soak up their habits (good or bad) just like a sponge. If someone you are associated with has habits that you don't want to pick up, you may want to separate yourself from that person.

7. WISE COUNSEL

Certain people can make anything seem right no matter how wrong it is. There are people who will use verses from the Bible to prove why it's okay to commit a crime. Be aware of the people that you seek counsel from, especially when you are on the fence about something life-changing.
Go to the older people with stability in their life. These people could include your parents, grandparents, teachers, and/or mentors.

8. THE GOLDEN RULE

Treat others in the same manner that you would like to be treated. REMEMBER: The point is for you to practice empathy, so put yourself in other people's shoes.

9. ASKING FOR HELP

There is no shame in asking for help. Especially when you've done all that you can do and used all of the resources available to you. Ask for the help you need and if you don't get the help from the first person, then go to the next until you find the help that you need.

CONSIDER THIS: We are all born into this world needing help and we would not have survived this far without it.

10. RIGHT OR WRONG

If you are not sure if something is right or wrong, just ask yourself, "Would the world be better or worse if everyone did this?" If the world would be worse or even unaffected, then you probably shouldn't be doing it. As a person of excellence or of good character, you want to do things that will be beneficial to this world.

MAKING GOOD DECISIONS

This section is designed to help you make better choices. Sometimes it's hard for us to make good choices because every decision is not always black or white. The tips below are designed to help you make good, everyday choices as well as handle those pesky gray areas. Although some people may accept the gray areas, that doesn't make them good choices. Look at the consequences of those actions: are they risky, unstable, dangerous, negative, or unhealthy? If they are, then you know that it's not for you. As a child of excellence, you want every decision you make to be a good one because you never know when it's the difference between life and death.

Another thing to consider about making good decisions is that we as people generally produce what we focus on. So, if you constantly focus on (or worry about) doing the "wrong thing" or making a "bad decision," then you probably will end up doing just that! So, instead, let's focus on simply doing what is right.

38 | TEEN SURVIVAL GUIDE

1. STAY CONSISTENT

It's often easier to do wrong than it is to do right. But doing wrong is like eating too much sweets, it tastes good for the moment but if eaten too often, it could cause major health issues (diabetes, cavities, obesity, etc.). Doing the right thing is a lot like exercise. If you do it once, you hardly see any results and you feel sore from doing it but if you continue to exercise you will become stronger, faster, healthier, and more confident. Consistency is the key.

2. BE PREPARED

If you can prepare for something, do it. You don't want to let life catch you off guard. Examples:

       (1) Studying just in case there is a pop quiz;
       (2) Keeping a spare tire in your car; or
       (3) Taking vitamins to prevent illness.

3. STRESS

Don't allow other people or anything to stress you. A lot of times we react negatively to certain things because it's been demonstrated to us. The good news is that just because you have the right to be stressed about something doesn't mean that you have to be.

If something unplanned happens and you feel the stress coming just think about what you can do to resolve the situation or at least to make it better. If you find that there's nothing that you can do, then do just that: nothing. Don't even get stressed.

4. DEALING WITH FRUSTRATION

When frustrated, we focus on the source of our frustration so much that we are blinded to everything else. When blinded by frustration it's easy to make poor or irrational decisions. To avoid this, you must make a decision RIGHT NOW to remain level-headed when frustrations arise.

CHALLENGE:
Try to sense when your frustration is arising so that you don't allow your emotions to take control but rather use your rational mind to resolve the problem.

5. DON'T QUIT

Never give up on doing the right thing. And don't be discouraged that sometimes people who are doing the wrong thing will seemingly find success faster than you. Keep in mind that most of the time they are more likely to lose their success just as fast or even faster because of the way they've gained it.

If you keep doing the right thing, you will eventually prosper, it will last forever, and no man on earth will be able to take it away. Find patience, and don't give up!

REMEMBER: Consistency is the key. Just like exercise, you can only see the results of your work when you stay consistent over time. So, stay consistent in well-doing, and you will see some overwhelming results in due time.

6. LEARN FROM YOUR MISTAKES

When you make a mistake or get in trouble, learn from it. That doesn't mean you should try to be sneakier next time. What it means is this: don't do what it is that got you in trouble in the first place.

Perhaps there is a better way to handle the situation. Analyze the situation and ask yourself, "What could I have done to avoid getting into trouble?" If you can't come up with an answer just as a parent, mentor, teacher, or pastor.

7. LEARNING FROM MISTAKES

It's good to learn from your mistakes, but don't stop there: learn from others' mistakes, too.

8. DON'T DO IT

If you don't know why you're doing something, don't do it. Think about what you do before you do it, and if it's not beneficial to yourself or anyone else, then don't do it. This can apply to many things. There is always some fad that seems cool for the moment but is not beneficial to your life.

9. MISSING OUT

For those of you who feel that you may be missing out on the thrills of life by making good choices, here is a list of a few things that you'll be glad that you're missing out on when you make good decisions:

- STDs or STIs;
- Prison/Jail time;
- Bad relationships;
- Unnecessary drama;
- Addictions;
- Uncontrollable anger;
- Hate in your heart;
- Lack of joy;
- Feeling empty inside, like part of you is missing; and
- Etc.

10. CHOOSE WISELY

Choose right over wrong at ALL TIMES: You never know when it will be a life or death decision. Sometimes peers try to make it seem like it's okay or normal to do wrong every now and then.

There have been people who have been on the right track to fulfilling their destiny. But they allowed someone to convince them to do wrong, and it cost them everything. Don't allow the same thing to happen to you.

11. REWARDS

No matter what you do in life, you will be rewarded for it, one way or the other. If you have good actions, your rewards will be pleasant and fulfilling. If you have bad actions, your reward will be uncomfortable and inconvenient.

STAYING
<u>FOCUSED</u>

How can we accomplish anything if we easily lose our focus? To stay focused, you need to know what your end goal is. Take the time to really think about the things that you want to accomplish in the near future, which are your short-term goals, and then think about the things that you'd like to accomplish within the next five years or so, which are your long-term goals. Once you have these written out, you have become a step closer to reaching them and becoming more focused.

If you plan to ignore this simple task of writing down your goals please know that when you have nothing to strive for, you end up wasting a lot of time doing foolish things or simply things that don't matter in the end. Basically, you end up just wasting your valuable time, or even worse, you could end up losing your time altogether. For example, making one poor decision could lead to prison, crippling injury, or even death.

44 | TEEN SURVIVAL GUIDE

This section is designed to help you stay focused on what's important instead of being distracted by the little things that at the end of the day, don't even matter.

1. DISTRACTIONS
Drama, fear, and jealousy are all examples of distractions designed to keep you from reaching your goals. I'm sure you could think of even more things that fall under this category. It's basically anything that doesn't add anything positive to your life.

CHALLENGE: The next time you are tempted to get wrapped up by drama, fear, or jealousy, just shift your mind to a positive focus. For example: Instead of getting reeled into drama, shift your focus to something more productive, like studying, sharpening a skill, looking for a job, starting your own business, or just focusing on your current short or long-term goal.

2. HOW TO INDULGE YOURSELF

Indulge yourself in positive things. If it's beneficial to your short-term and long-term goals then it's worth spending time on. It's a waste of time to indulge in negative things such as gossip and slander. These things can not only waste your time but can also have extremely negative consequences.

3. ARGUING

We try so often to prove people wrong that we miss our opportunity to do things right. Stay focused on what you should be doing. Arguments are a distraction. Most of the time it's best to let things go. Even if you are right and they are wrong, is it worth your time to try to convince someone who will never change their mind anyway? It's not.

4. PEOPLE OF FAITH

If you are religious or a person of faith, your lifestyle should reflect your faith. If it doesn't, that means that you are not focusing on the right things. If this is you, then you need to shift your focus.

5. PATIENCE

Anything that's worth having is worth waiting for. When going after your dreams or when in pursuit of your destiny, you need patience because most of the time reaching your goals requires waiting.

If you don't learn how to wait on your own, life will teach you over time. So as you are staying focused on your goals remember that waiting is just part of the process to your success.

RELATIONSHIPS

You will have many relationships in your life, from friendships to romantic relationships and even professional relationships. These tips are designed to help you develop and improve your current and future relationships.

1. MAKING FRIENDS
Don't waste time trying to be like anyone else. If you stay true to your personality, you will attract others that you can relate to.

2. WATCH WHAT YOU SAY
When you don't know what to say, sometimes it's best to not say anything at all. Let your actions speak for you.

3. STAY PROTECTED
Just like a fence around a house, we must keep our morals and boundaries up. Otherwise, anything or anyone could invade us or influence us. Apply this to the music you listen to, what you watch, and even the people you associate yourself with.

4. DOMESTIC VIOLENCE
Boys and Girls should not be hitting each other or provoking one to hit the other. Both are wrong but not equally.

Due to double standards, it is considered worse for a boy to hit a girl and I agree with this because women are precious to human existence. If you don't think so, just remember that it was a woman who birthed you into this world.

Boys: If a girl hits you, protect yourself without hitting her. Even if you have to run away, do NOT hit her back. Once you get away, alert an authority figure (whoever is in charge).

Girls: If a boy hits you, don't try to make excuses for him or put the blame onto yourself. Please know that you don't ever deserve for anyone to hit you. If it happens, alert the authorities immediately. And if you are in a relationship with that person, end it immediately and never return, otherwise, you are giving him permission to hit you again.

5. LAUGHTER

Laughing is medicine for the soul, but keep this in mind, laughing at something is like saying, "I agree with that." For example: If someone is making jokes about someone you know, and you laugh, you become just as guilty as the person who originally made the joke in the eyes of the person being laughed at.

REMEMBER:

A cheap laugh is always at someone else's expense. You don't have to be doing wrong to have a good time.

6. THE LACK-OF-LOVE EFFECT

Do not be a victim of the lack of love effect. When we feel the lack of love from the people who are important to us (usually parents), we as humans seem to subconsciously seek that love elsewhere.

For some, that means joining a gang, becoming prematurely sexually active, or doing wrong just to get attention from those who are seemingly ignoring you. These are all choices that always end up bringing more confusion and even more pain in your life. Now that you know the symptoms you can stop yourself from being a victim of the Lack-of-Love Effect.

7. LOVE

What good is being famous, having fans, and all of the money in the world if you don't have love? I'm talking about the love that enables you to forgive your enemy or the love that allows you to give to people in need. Focus on love.

8. ALONE TIME

Sometimes we get lonely because we don't have anyone to talk to or hang out with. So, instead of focusing on your loneliness, enjoy the time you have to yourself. Use that time to better yourself so that when you do spend time with people you'll have more to offer and maybe even something new to talk about.

9. DATING

Dating began as a way to get to know someone who could potentially become your future spouse. So, if you are looking to get married in the next 3-5 years, it's a good idea to start dating. But, if you don't plan to get married anytime soon, then why date? Why invest time, money, and emotions into something that you are not even committed to?

It's very likely that the other person will develop feelings for you, and if you don't want a relationship, it will end in heartache, pain, and regret, and leave you both with emotional baggage.

10. LOANING MONEY

It's true that it's better to give than to receive. So, if a friend wants to borrow money from you, and you have enough, why not give it to him or her?

However, you need to know that loans between friends can cause strife and confusion and even ruin the relationship. That's why I suggest that if you can afford to, just give it to your friend instead of loaning them the money but if you are not in a position to give money as a gift, it's better that you don't give it at all.

11. HAPPINESS

If you depend on others to make you happy, you'll never be satisfied. Your happiness is your responsibility. It's not fair to put that on someone else.

12. LOVED

Every person that you see means something to someone, and, believe it or not, you are very dear to someone's heart as well. Treat people like they are valuable, and don't forget that you are valuable too.

13. BLAME GAME

When something goes wrong, do you make excuses or blame others first? Instead of blaming others, consider what you could have done differently, or consider that you could be the problem.

When you do this, you will grow more mature and others will be more understanding of your situation when you admit your faults, which is the first step towards fixing them. This will also help you to be more understanding of others when they make mistakes.

14. BLAME GAME II

When something goes missing, and the first thing you ask someone is, "Did you take…" or "Did you steal…?" That's not good.

When you react that way, you could easily damage a healthy friendship. Instead, ask if they've seen what you're looking for and if they say no, don't keep asking them as if you are interrogating them. Instead, just give them the benefit of the doubt.

In other words, just trust them. It's a bad feeling when you blame someone for stealing something and then realize that you just misplaced what you were looking for.

15. KNOW YOURSELF FIRST
In order to have a healthy relationship, you need to first know who you are. For instance, if you know that you have major self-esteem issues, then you know that it's not a good idea for you to get into a romantic relationship until you become more secure.

16. RESPECT OTHERS PROPERTY
Treat people's things just as good as or better than you treat your things. By doing this, you are more likely to maintain that relationship and the ability to borrow their things in the future.

54 | TEEN SURVIVAL GUIDE

PARENTS

When we're born, we don't get to choose where we're from, our name, or even what family we're born into. With that being said, we have to make the best of whatever our situation is.

As a young adult, it is perfectly normal to be annoyed by your parents. That doesn't make you a bad person. However, you must be mindful not to allow small annoyances to cause you to behave in a way that could ruin your relationship with your parents.

There are adults out there who haven't spoken to their parents in years because of something they may have said when they were just a teenager. There are other worse scenarios when the parent dies before they reconcile their issues.

The following tips are strategies to make living with your parents more bearable and less aggravating.

56 | TEEN SURVIVAL GUIDE

1. PARENTS
Even if your parents are mean, rude, and unfair to you, they are still your parents. So, for your own sake, respect and honor them anyway. Don't even speak negatively about them to others. All that does is open the door for others to do the same. REMEMBER: There is no benefit to being disrespectful to your parents.

2. MAKE YOURSELF VALUABLE
As a teenager, within the next 1 to 5 years, you may be moving out of your parents' house. So, while you are still there you should be an asset and not a burden. To be an asset, you can do things like cook, clean, take out the trash, and do yard work. When you clean, also clean up after other people, including your parents.

When you cook, don't just cook for yourself, cook for the whole family. Do things that help relieve your parents of extra stress and aggravation like saving them money on energy bills.

When you do these things, don't look at it as a burden, look at it as an investment. If you do this now, when you move out, you will be missed. If you are missed, your parents will be more likely to help you when you need them. Just so you know, it is very likely that you will need their help.

KEEP THIS IN MIND:
If you don't usually help around the house, it's likely that you will be accused of doing good deeds to get something in return or even hiding something.
This tip will only work in your favor if you:
(1) Don't ask for anything big in the near future and
(2) Stay consistent with helping out.

3. AGGRAVATING PARENTS

Even when they get on your nerves, don't forget that your parents love you. Even when they constantly remind you of your mistakes, remember that they still love you. For those of you who don't have your biological parents in your lives, please don't develop hate in your hearts toward them. Instead, just appreciate the parents or guardians that you do have in your life that much more.

4. PARENTS ARE HUMANS TOO

Don't forget that your parents are human and that they will make mistakes. When they do, forgive them and give them a chance to redeem themselves. Why not? Don't you want them to do the same for you? REMEMBER: Forgiveness is not always given to those who deserve it nor does it always benefit them. But, it will always benefit you, the forgiver.

5. YOU ARE NOT ALONE
There is nothing new under the sun when it comes to human interaction and relationships.
In other words, the things that you are going through now are not new. People have been going through the same things for thousands of years.

Right now, there are millions who are going through the same situations that you are, and, just like you, they are not sharing their pain with anyone. If you are feeling alone, talk to someone, preferably a mentor or a parent. You'll be surprised who can relate to your problems.

REMEMBER: Good parents and mentors are always seeking new ways to help you and to be a part of your life. If you know that you have a good parent or guardian, then reach out to them with your problems.

ANGER

This section can help you handle your anger and even prevent you from making bad choices while angry. Just remember that it is normal to get mad occasionally, but anger should not be anyone's normal condition. When it is, you will suffer due to your own actions.

So, what is anger? I think we can all agree that anger is a passionate emotion usually seen in people with big hearts. Anger is one of the most powerful of your emotions and the one that's most likely to lead you to do something that you'll later regret. Staying in a state of anger is even physically bad for you. People who stay in a state of anger are more likely to develop illnesses at a much higher rate than a positive person.

What we have to remember (even into adulthood) is that we have the power to determine how we respond to our feelings. Everything that you do goes through your mind before you do it. For example, if someone calls you ugly, your emotions may tell you to punch them in the face, but the action of punching them has to be approved by your mind before it can take place.

Now, I am not totally against getting mad. When something makes you mad, that usually indicates that there has been some level of injustice, which, in turn, helps you realize that something needs to change or be adjusted. Anger can be someone's motivation to do something creative like invent something that fixes a major problem. For example, I imagine that the person who invented the elevator was fed up with constantly walking up flights of stairs, especially after a long day.

Ultimately, anger can drive one to take action. You can use anger as your fuel to do something positive. I realize that what I'm saying may sound radical to some because, when angry, you are less likely to make good choices but keep in mind that you are in control of the decisions you make, not your anger.

1. FUEL TO THE FIRE
Every time you tell the story of how someone did you wrong, you are subconsciously reliving that same pain over again! Even though it can be good to let off some steam every now and then, but when you overdo it, that's when you're just adding fuel to the fire.

Unless you are trying to find a solution to the problem, don't waste time talking about it.

2. LIKE A PUPPET
Try not to allow someone else's actions to determine your actions. For example, just because someone gets an attitude with you doesn't mean that you have to get one back. Beware of this because some people use your anger to control you, just like a puppet. I've actually overheard people say things like, "Watch this, I'm going to make him/her mad." Then they would say something that they knew would make the person upset. Do you want someone to have that kind of power over you? If not, take control of your emotions.

CONSIDER THIS: When someone does something to intentionally make you angry, don't immediately retaliate (or react). Look at the situation and make sure the actions you take are beneficial to the situation.

Example: "A girl walks up to you and calls you ugly." Don't just react based on what she says.

Think about it.

Will your anger change anything?

Maybe she really believes that you are ugly and if that's true, will getting mad change her opinion?

Or maybe she is just being offensive to get a reaction from you?

After thinking about it you may respond by smiling and saying something like, "I'm sorry you feel that way because I think that you are beautiful." or you may decide to not respond at all.

Whatever you do, make sure that you stay in control of your emotions and not allow yourself to be controlled by anyone else.

3. JUST A MISTAKE

Have you ever accidentally made anyone angry or offended them with something you said or did? Consider that the next time you get angry with someone. Sometimes people don't realize what they are doing. It's okay to let things go, especially if someone didn't mean to offend you.

4. PEACE

Find something productive that brings you peace and hold on tightly to it. That way, when you are angry, you can channel that anger by doing what brings you peace.

Be sure that the activity that brings you peace is productive and wholesome, like playing an instrument, participating in sports, drawing, writing, or singing.

5. GRUDGES

Holding on to a grudge is like carrying luggage: the more you have, the harder it is to make it to your destination. Whenever you travel, it costs you more when you have extra luggage, and it's the same in life. The question is: "What is your baggage costing you?"

CHALLENGE:

Make a list of all of your grudges, and then make a decision to forgive everyone on the list.

6. EXTREMES

Try not to go from one extreme to the next. For example, if a teacher tells you that you are talking too much, don't get so mad that you just stop talking altogether. All that's going to do is cause more confusion when they ask you a question and you don't respond.

Likewise, if a peer sees you smiling and says something like, "Why are you always smiling so hard?" Don't just stop smiling altogether and start walking around looking mad. All that's going to do is cause someone else to ask, "What are you so sad?" And your response will probably be, "First, they didn't like that I was smiling; now they wondering why I'm not! I just can't please these people!"

The fact is, you literally can't please everyone. So, instead of trying to please everyone based solely on their comments, just be yourself. Don't get me wrong, it's okay to take advice. Just try not to take it to the extreme.

7. MAD DECISIONS

Try not to make any major decisions while angry. Instead, wait until you calm down and you are thinking logically before making any major decisions.

Making decisions while angry can easily lead to regret. While angry, we tend to lose focus on what's really important and we respond based on how we feel at that moment. Then, after we've made our bad decision(s), we feel guilty because we said or did things that don't reflect our true character.

8. WATCH YOUR MOUTH

When angry, especially toward people you love, try not to speak irrationally. You may end up saying something that you'll regret. If you must speak, choose your tone wisely. It's not always about what you say but how you say it. This is important on a daily basis, too, even when you're not angry.

9. CONSEQUENCES OF WORDS

Think about the consequences of your words before speaking. You can choose your words but you can't choose the consequences. Even though someone may forgive you for what you've said, you can't unsay it, and they can't unhear it.

10. STAY IN PEACE

Although you may lose control over a situation you don't have to lose control over yourself.

CHALLENGE: If this is an area that you struggle in, then tell yourself every day that you will not lose control over your emotions the next time the opportunity presents itself. Doing this will increase your chances of success. Believe in yourself, you can do this.

11. PRESSURE

Sometimes we feel weight or pressure from our responsibilities and sometimes it gets so bad (or heavy) that we feel as if we are carrying around a boulder.

Imagine struggling all day carrying a boulder and someone comes by and says something as simple as, "Hey, how are you doing?" Because of the pressure from your boulder (or situation) your response may resemble this: "Don't you see this boulder weighing me down? How do think I'm doing?"

What we sometimes fail to realize is that other people don't see our boulders (or our problems). So, we should try our best not to take our pain out on others. I understand that you have a lot to deal with, but that has nothing to do with anyone but yourself.

If you've recently taken your frustrations out on someone you should immediately apologize to them. No need to let your problems create even more problems.

12. GETTING OVER ANGER
A very effective way to get over being angry is by being kind to others. Anger can be due to selfishness, so by showing generosity, you can negate that anger.

CHALLENGE:
The next time you are angry, go out of your way to be kind to everyone that you can.

BULLYING

Have you ever heard the saying, "Hurting people, hurt people"? Well, it's true. Sometimes a bully is a victim of some form of pain or injustice. Although this does not justify the pain they cause, it does help us to understand them better. Being able to empathize with one another makes it easier for us to coexist.

With that being said, some people are just mean-spirited. Those people are seeking a reaction. That reaction could be fear, sadness, or even anger. When dealing with those people, we can't give them the reaction that they're looking for. We must not allow their negative actions to determine our actions. When they see that they can't steal your joy, it's likely that they'll leave you alone.

Although there are many real bullies out there, sometimes we feel bullied when we shouldn't. Sometimes we are just being overly sensitive. On the other hand, sometimes we are the bullies when we don't mean to be. It's easy to get caught up in the moment trying to make your peers laugh and end up hurting someone's feelings. This section is designed to help you stop being a bully and prevent you from becoming a bully's victim.

1. BE YOURSELF

If you are goofy, be goofy. If you are nerdy, be nerdy. No matter who you are, be yourself. Don't change your actions because someone calls you a name. If you like to laugh and someone calls you goofy, don't try to be more serious. Your goofiness is what makes you awesome! Try to develop a boldness that says, "Yeah, I'm goofy. So you better get used to it!"

REMEMBER: Even if someone doesn't particularly like your goofiness, they'll respect your boldness.

2. HATERS

It's a waste of time trying to understand why haters hate you. Sometimes people just hate you for no reason at all, and there is nothing that you could have done to prevent it.

Think about it like this: there are some foods you won't like no matter who cooks them. It doesn't have to be personal, and it shouldn't stop you from eating. In the same way, some people just won't like you no matter what you do, and it should not stop you from being yourself and living life to the fullest.

3. SILENCE

It's not always necessary to argue or shout just to prove a point. Sometimes silence is more powerful than your words. Sometimes, the people arguing against you will prove your point for you while they're shouting and yelling without you having to say anything.

4. RESPECT YOURSELF

If you want people to respect you, first respect yourself. Never speak ill of or about yourself. All that does is give people permission to treat you just as badly. Carry yourself as the person you are on the inside. Also, when you speak badly about yourself, most of the time it just makes the people around you feel uncomfortable.

CHALLENGE:
The next time you have a negative thought about yourself, replace it with something positive instead.

5. MOVING FORWARD

Sometimes we can be going about our day and someone could say one thing that ruins our good mood for the rest of the day and we end up soaking in our sorrows.

I implore you to get up and move forward. Be strong, and push through your emotions! Don't allow someone else's actions to determine how you feel.

CONSIDER THIS: Think about your future goals for the next 5-10 years. What would the successful future you tell yourself? Would the future you say about this problem that you have now? Will it even matter in the next few years or months or days? If not, let it go and move on!

6. PITTY PARTY

If you constantly put yourself down, who would bother picking you up? Downing yourself does not help people feel sorry for you, but, instead, it opens the door for people to put you down even further.

7. THE POWER OF KINDNESS

One of the most powerful things that you can do is be nice to someone who has been mean to you. It will blow their mind.

8. TOUGH SKIN

To develop tough skin you must constantly remind yourself of who you are:

SMART
KIND
TALENTED
 and OVERALL AMAZING!

Remind yourself of this every day so that when people tell you otherwise, you don't take it to heart. But, instead, you let it bounce off of your tough skin.

CHALLENGE:
Make a list of good qualities that describe you or that you want to describe you, and read it every day until it sinks in.

9. SEPARATE YOURSELF

If you are a person who has friends who get you into trouble and jeopardize your safety, then those are not true friends. Separate yourself from people who could delay or prevent you from reaching your goals. It may seem hurtful to just cut people off all at once, so consider slowly removing yourself from the picture.

10. STICKS AND STONES

Sticks and stones may break your bones, and if you allow them, words can hurt, too. So, I implore you to guard your hearts. Just let the negativity go in one ear and out of the other.

CONSIDER THIS:

If a random person whom you don't know approached you and said, "I don't like you!" You probably wouldn't care. But, if one of your parents said the same thing, then it would probably hurt or scar you. The reason why is because your parents have a special place in your heart while a random person doesn't. My point is, don't just let anyone have your heart. Not everyone knows or even cares how to handle it.

11. FIGHTING FIRE WITH FIRE?

Who would try to put out a fire with gas? In the same way, we can't fight fire with fire or fight evil with evil. We must fight fire with water and evil with love. Fight bullying with sincere compliments. Fight anger with peace.

CHALLENGE:
Intentionally be nice to everyone who has been mean to you.

SEX

It is normal to be curious about sex as a teenager, but society will make it seem normal to be sexually active as a teenager. Don't be fooled. Society is not concerned about your personal life, and they don't tell you all of the problems and risks that come along with having sex prematurely.

People will tell you that if you just use protection you will be okay. However, that is not completely true. Although condoms can protect you from becoming pregnant or from catching a disease, they sometimes fail to work properly. Condoms can break.

It is my goal to be open and honest with you when it comes to having sex prematurely. I will share with you some of the risks of being sexually active as well as the benefits of waiting.

THE RISKS OF SEX

Below is a list of potential problems to beware of when it comes to premature sex whether you are male, female, gay, or straight.

1. STI/STD:

Every time you have sex with someone, you are making yourself susceptible to a vast number of sexually transmitted infections and/or diseases. Here are just a few:

Gonorrhea

Herpes

HPV

Chlamydia

Crabs

REMEMBER: No STD or STI is pleasant and some of them are even permanent (lasts forever). It is also worth stating that people who have STDs or more likely to get HIV/AIDS which in most cases has been deadly.

2. Pregnancy:

This can be stressful for boys and girls, Physically, financially, and emotionally. Some even have to drop out of school and miss out on a real childhood. Having a child could set you back anywhere from 5-25 years when it comes to reaching your goals.

3. Child Support:
Females: Having to go through the process of making someone take care of your baby that they don't want or just can't afford. This can not only be stressful but also heartbreaking and traumatic. Imagine having to force someone to care for a baby that they helped you to create.

Males: Imagine having to pay money you don't have when you are already doing the best you can to care for your new baby. Or imagine just being taken advantage of. Let's face it, everyone on child support is NOT a deadbeat dad. Sometimes people get scared that you could back out at any moment and want to secure their finances at your expense. Keep in mind, in some states, if you don't pay, you are put in jail and still responsible for the payments that should have been made while you were in jail.

4. Emotional Stress:
Typically speaking, teens aren't emotionally mature enough

to be sexually active. This means that you will have to go through EXTRA strife, confusion, and unnecessary stress due to unhealthy relationships. This could lead to abuse, physical and verbal fights, manipulation, and so much more.

5. Becoming addicted:
Becoming prematurely sexually active could cause you to lose focus of everything! You know that someone is addicted to sex when the only thing that they focus on is the opportunity to have sex again. This can cause major issues in every aspect of your life (your education, finances, relationships, religion, self-esteem, peace, etc.)

6. Being used, only for your body:
It's not fun being used, especially when it's by the person that you care for. Some will only call you when they want sex from you, but when you call or need their help with anything else, they're nowhere to be found. Some will even refuse to help you when you're in need unless you offer them some form of sex in return. You are worth more than that and when you are caught up you can easily find your-

self as this kind of victim.

7. Ruined reputation:
Females: You could get the reputation of being a whore, tramp, slut, or Jezebel just because you had sex one time. People tend to choose to believe the juicy gossip or the worst about people over the truth. Boys talk and some will slander your name just to make themselves look good.

Males: You could develop the reputation as the type of guy who just hits and quits or even someone who is bad in bed. Sometimes your partner will claim that you took advantage of them just to keep themselves out of trouble, which could put you in jail or attacked by one of their loved ones. Remember: Just because it's not true, doesn't mean that you won't be treated like it is true.

8. Abandonment:
Sometimes people get sex from you and never talk to you again and even pretend that they don't know you anymore. Sometimes you never even find out why.

9. Domestic Violence:
You could end up in an emotionally and/or physically abusive relationship. This sometimes happens when someone feels like they own you because you had sex with them.

They could even develop extreme jealousy (which is sometimes misplaced). Keep in mind, that abusive people don't always appear to be that way early in the relationship. Sometimes, you don't find out until sex is involved.

10. Being negatively influenced:
Sometimes people will use sex to convince (or bribe) you to do things that are dangerous, illegal, and overall something that you wouldn't normally do which could cost you your reputation, your health, your freedom, or your life. You have to ask yourself, is it worth it?

11. Developing Trust and Self-esteem issues:
People could stop trusting you due to multiple lies derived from your sex life. You could also develop misplaced trust issues toward family members and friends because you compared them to those who hurt you in the past. This could also affect your future relationships and possibly keep you from getting close enough to anyone to make a real connection that transcends beyond sex.

12. Emotionally disconnecting with others (especially parents):

The guilt that comes with premarital sex could make you very distant from those who love you, all because you know that it would disappoint them if they knew that you were sexually active. This could cause permanent rifts in the relationship and constant awkwardness with someone who once made you feel safe.

13. Developing Emotional Scars and Baggage:
After your relationship is over and you've moved on to someone else, you could carry issues from your previous relationship to the new one. Bringing old baggage from past relationships pretty much ruins the new relationship before it even has a chance to begin.

14. False Sense of Security:
Using condoms does NOT guarantee that you will not get an STI/STD or become pregnant.

You may also feel a false sense of security when you think that someone can't or won't leave you because you had sex with them. Don't fall into the trap! Sometimes people will say anything just to get sex from you. They could say that they are in love with you and want to marry you someday then after they have sex with you, they just leave.

15. Pressure:
Sometimes people will attempt to pressure you into sex. They'll attempt to make you feel guilty in order to get what they want from you. For example, They may say things like, "You'll do it if you really love me!" Don't fall in the trap!

16. Sex can blind you:
Becoming blinded by sex means that you are so indulged in sex that everything else doesn't seem to matter, and it causes you to miss important details about the person that you are involved with.

The sex could easily blind you to all of that person's personality flaws. Without sex, you'll take more notice of the finer details in what they say and how they treat you, which are more important in the end.

It's heartbreaking when your relationship ends and you've missed all of the clues that should have told you that the person wasn't right for you because you were blinded by sex.

KEEP YOUR VIRGINITY

If you are a virgin, I implore you to stay a virgin until you get married. It may seem hard to do in this society, but it will be well worth it on so many levels (physically, emotionally, mentally, financially, and spiritually). If you already lost your virginity it's not too late to start over by becoming celibate, meaning that you refuse to have sex again until you're married. It's not too late to gain some of the benefits of waiting until marriage before having sex.

HOW TO STAY CELIBATE

Remember that your thoughts are the foundation of your actions. So, if or when you begin to think about anything sexual or even sex-related, purposely change your focus. Remember that you have control over your thoughts and that you are strong enough to think about things other than sex. Also, NEVER allow yourself to be alone with someone you will be tempted to have sex with. Even when dating in hopes of finding a spouse, don't spend extended periods alone with them. All of your dates should be in public places or in the company of others. Not only does this help you to stay out of temptation, but you also get the opportunity to see how your potential mate interacts with other people and how they treat you in the presence of others. Celibacy is a beautiful thing, it really helps.

THE BENEFITS OF WAITING

I've said previously that the best things are worth waiting for and that also includes sex. So, the list below is some benefits to preserving your virginity and remaining celibate.

1. Reputation
People who choose to be virgins are usually respected and trusted more by most people. Also, it feels good to know that no one knows anything about you sexually who could compromise your reputation.

2. No guilt
It is freeing when you know that you don't have anything to hide or be ashamed of.

3. Physical health
Not having to constantly worry about whether you have an STD/STI. You also don't have to worry about being pregnant or getting someone else pregnant.

THINK ABOUT THIS: When everyone around you who is sexually active, finds out that there has been a major outbreak of a particular STD or STI, you won't have to question if you have it because you have not been sexually active.

4. Emotional clarity
When you are not sexually active you don't have to worry about emotional attachments to people you know aren't good for you. You also don't have to worry about becoming blinded by sex.

5. Mindsets
Having the mindset to stay a virgin or celibate protects you from developing poor mentalities, such as thinking that every person in a relationship cheats or that sex is the only thing that's worth having from your partner.

6. Success
When you are not distracted by sex, you are able to focus on things that are more beneficial to your future, such as your education, networking, sharpening your skills, and even securing your finances.

7. Reassurance
When you get married, you won't have to question if your partner truly loves you because you've already connected with your partner on a much deeper level than sex. Because

of this, your marriage will be more likely to succeed.

CONSIDER THIS:
When you finally get married, the sex will be much more frequent than people who started their relationship having sex.

CONCLUSION

If you find something that is beneficial in the book, please share it with others. These tips are not secrets, neither are they hidden gems. They have always been available to those who seek them.

Even though some tips were thought of by way of my own mistakes or even my own successes, a vast majority of the tips in this book did not originate from my own thoughts or experiences. They've developed from so many sources over the years (from childhood to adulthood).

So, I'd like to give a very special thanks to everyone who has ever imparted any wisdom to me, especially my parents. A lot of the tips in this book are biblical too, so I thank God for that! Some tips were inspired by quotes that I've heard but didn't know who said it. So, to the unknown people who said those quotes that stuck with me, thank you for putting positivity into this world. You are truly appreciated.

90 | TEEN SURVIVAL GUIDE

I have one final tip that I'd like to give which is not an original quote but it is very true and I have seen it in my life and in the lives of others.

FINAL TIP:
Whatever you seek, you will find, and whatever you feed will grow. So, seek good things and feed yourself with positivity, truth, and love.

In conclusion, I will end this book in the same way that I used to end all of my classes. Which was by saying the following,

"Happy to see you come, sad to see you go! Have a great day! See you next time."

www.ingramcontent.com/pod-product-compliance
Lightning Source LLC
Chambersburg PA
CBHW050604300426
44112CB00013B/2065